THE BEAST OF THE APOCALYPSO.

& Other Risible Irreverencies from the pages of

Books & Religion

B&R PRESS
Trinity Church
New York
1990

INTRODUCTION

It may be asked why a periodical called **Books & Religion** has made such an effort to publish, and now to collect, cartoons?

What's funny about religion, or the books that religion generates? On the other hand (our questioner might go on), we have a magazine, full of cartoons, called *The New Yorker*. What's funny about New York?

Well, plenty, of course. And there are funny things about religion. In fact, those who have hung around religious institutions long enough to learn both what they have to teach and how miserably they fail to live up to their teachings are reminded of two other institutions: the government, and the academy.

The government is nakedly about money and power, though its rhetoric is often more exalted, and its form of politics—real politics—is often straightforward to the point of crudity. The academy and the church and synagogue, however, are institutions that claim to be about something more important, something higher—truth itself. That's what makes them funnier than government. And at least as absurd.

Many of the cartoons that you are about to encounter in the pages which follow have nothing directly to do with religion or religious institutions. On the other hand, God is plainly interested in things other than religion, and some of them are funny too, like flatulance and penguins and bishops.

It can be argued that a cartoon has no more need for a defense than does a sunset or a sneeze. They make sense, and form our world. As Oscar Wilde wrote, "Life imitates art." Those of us who love cartoons have seen situations that remind us of favorite cartoonists. If certain family tragedies remind us of Dostoevski, certain office situations or garage sales might remind us of, for example, P.S. Mueller—and so do certain family tragedies.

There is another connection between religion and humor that ought to be noted, because it is so frequently suffered. Some ministers, priests, and rabbis feel the need to start their sermons off with a little joke. This is frequently a painful exercise; you can even find, in some magazines you wouldn't want to read (God knows, **Books & Religion** isn't one of them) advertisements for books full of jokes clergymen can tell, and it makes your flesh crawl to think that you may actually at some point be on the receiving end. What is most predictable, and always appalling, is that at the end of the exercise the minister, priest, or rabbi, having (if they are lucky) gotten a laugh, will say, when the last polite chuckle has subsided, "But you know, there is a profound *truth* here."

Let us reassure you: there is no profound truth here. Not in this book.And if any of these cartoons end up in a sermon we will be profoundly disappointed. Even a tad annoyed. Which is why **Books & Religion** has on its staff a large man with a thick neck and no sense of humor at all. It is his job to make it clear to readers who fail to heed our admonition that his ways are not their ways. He will not tolerate any abuse of these cartoons. He knows that you have bought this book, and he is ever vigilant. This is his only job. And don't even think about joking your way out of this one. You've been warned. Find your laughter here and your sermons somewhere else. Or else.

The Editors
Books & Religion
New York City, November 1990

WE BELIEVE IN YOU!
I WILL NEVER MAKE A FIST.
MVELLER

2

Ahab and Moby, right before things got out of hand.

FATHER O'LEARY EXERCISING THE DEMONS

SEDUCED BY TECHNOLOGY.

"DON'T THINK TOO MUCH."
HMM... WONDER WHAT HE'S *REALLY* TRYING TO SAY...
KIRK ©89

THE FILING CABINET
OF THE GODS.
LIFE
DEATH
MISC.
MUELLER

"Hey! Why the long faces? C'mon, everybody... LIGHTEN UP!"

GODOT WAITING FOR HIS LUGGAGE.
FLIGHTS
MUELLER

Senior Investment Analyst R.J. Thornhill glimpses the Universe in a grain of sand and is not impressed.

THE GOD OF WHAT-NOTS AND BRIC-A-BRAC.
GOTTA BUILD SOME SHELVES.
MUELLER

OK, all you hot-shot, wise-guy philosophy buffs... here's one for you (and it's good for 15 extra-credit points):

If a tree falls in a forest, partially filling a drinking glass, is the glass:
a) half-empty, or
b) half-full?

GLASS
TREE

Please keep your eyes on your own work. Thank you.

VENDING MACHINES IN HELL   KIRK ©89

BAD
IDEAS

THE NEW IDS ON THE BLOCK.

MUELLER

SHRINK WRAP.

CAN I
ACCEPT THIS?
MUELLER

FOLK WISDOM OF THE GALAXIES

THE WAITING ROOM IN SECULAR HEAVEN.
MUELLER

PASSING ACQUAINTANCE WITH THE TRUTH...
NO, DON'T TELL ME... LET ME GUESS. I NEVER FORGET A FACE! IT WAS 2 YEARS AGO, MALIBU, A LUNCH THING, RIGHT?
VELEY

What separates Man from the animals is his capacity to rationalize.

BAD IDEAS

POSTMODERN HUMOR.

P.S. MUELLER

PARANOID
OPEN DOOR POLICY.
MUELLER

Guarded optimism.

THE MEEK
INHERIT THE
POWERLESS.
MUELLER

NO HELP FOR THE SNEERING IMPAIRED.
MUELLER

"Can I call you right back? I seem to have some
kind of identity-crisis thing happening here!"

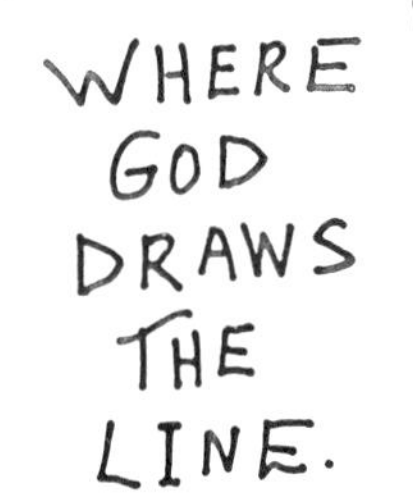

WHERE
GOD
DRAWS
THE
LINE.

BLENDERS FOR THE BLENDERLESS!

BALLAST
FOR THE
WEIGHTLESS.

SMALLTALK FOR
THE SPEECHLESS.

FEATURES FOR THE
FEATURELESS.

FECK
FOR THE
FECKLESS.

P.S. MUELLER

IT'S A RARE
FORM OF
MARXISM.
MUELLER

Marty decides to become a friend of Planet Earth:

SHIRLEY MACLAINE IN HER CAMBRIAN PERIOD.
MUELLER

ATTENTION SPAN REMAINING:
3 27
MINS. SECS.
VELEY

Really Harold.
That's rather
petty.
KIRK ©89

FAITH HEALING
FOR
SINUS TROUBLE.

MEBBE I SHOULD BE FENCED IN!
MUELLER
SELF DOUBT IN THE OLD WEST.

"I'll let you in on a little secret, son. If you're really, *really* careful, absolute power only corrupts a little bit!"

DEATH WITHOUT DIGNITY.
SIMUELLER

WHERE DOES IT ALL GO?
THE ASHCAN OF HISTORY
THE TRASH-COMPACTOR OF SOCIOLOGY
THE SOLID-WASTE LANDFILL OF POLITICAL SCIENCE
VELEY

GERALDO MUD WRESTLES THE DEVIL HIMSELF.
MUELLER

"Larry, you have everything it takes to go far in this company, but a word of advice: lose the laugh."

BAD IDEAS
TWIN PEEKS.
P.S. MUELLER

"IN THE NEXT HALF HOUR, MY WEALTHY WHITE CONSERVATIVE MALE FRIENDS AND I WILL DISCUSS THE ANNOYINGLY PERSISTENT BLACK UNDER-CLASS, AND WHY WOMEN GET SO EMOTIONAL ABOUT ABORTION."

THE LORD WORKS IN MYSTERIOUS WAYS.
MUELLER

The day after the meek inherit the Earth.

HERE'S WHAT PEOPLE ARE SAYING ABOUT

CULTS, INC.®

CARLOTTA P., AKRON, OH:

"YOU'RE DARNED TOOTIN'! CULTS, INC.® UNLOCKED MY LEADERSHIP POTENTIAL IN WAYS I NEVER DREAMED OF! WITH THEIR HELP, PROFESSIONAL GUIDANCE AND EASY-TO-READ INSTRUCTIONS, I TRANSFORMED MY DOTTY OLD BRIDGE CLUB INTO A THRIVING CULT WITH 14 CHAPTERS AND MORE ON THE WAY! AND WHAT A SWEET LITTLE MONEY-MAKER! $68,425 LAST MONTH, AND THAT'S AFTER-TAX NET, MIND YOU!"

PETER T., SAN LUIS OBISPO, CA:

"I'VE ALWAYS BEEN PARTIAL TO FLASHY COSTUMES, SECRET PASS-WORDS AND THE ROAR OF FRENZIED, IRRATIONAL MOBS, BUT I NEVER HAD THE CONFIDENCE TO GO OUT ON MY OWN. WELL, CULTS INC.® SURE CHANGED ALL THAT! I'VE UNLEASHED MESMERIZING, CROWD-ELECTRIFYING CHARISMA I NEVER KNEW I HAD! AND THE MONEY!! I'M ABSOLUTELY ROLLING IN THE STUFF!! YOU CAN BE TOO!"

JOHN D., TULLYTOWN, PA:

"I DON'T LIKE CROWDS, NEVER HAVE. NATURALLY, I HAD ALWAYS ASSUMED I WASN'T CULT MATERIAL. WELL, CULTS, INC.® SHOWED ME HOW WRONG I WAS! THROUGH "SINGLE PROPRIETOR CULT INCORPORATION" I'M EARNING MORE MONEY THAN I CAN COUNT, IN MY SPARE TIME! HERE'S A LIST OF MY ACTUAL BANK DEPOSITS (THIS COULD BE YOU!):"

JAN: $22,634		FEB: $28,374	
MAR: $31,023		APRIL: $42,442 (!)	
MAY: $39,203		JUNE: $49,968 (!!)	

VELEY

TRANSENDENTAL VEGETATION.
MUELLER

BAD
IDEAS

RAISING EYEBROWS

P.S. MUELLER

"I don't know what's wrong with me... It's getting so I can't tell the difference between the Truth and a truism anymore!"

I TRY NOT TO READ EVERYTHING I BELIEVE.
LIES
LIES
LIES
LIES
MUELLER

"Taking it with you is actually pretty easy. The trick is finding a place up here where you can spend it!"

BAD
IDEAS
MIME WARP.
P.S. MUELLER

"If you've read any *Zen* at all, Fred, you'll know that I did not stab you in the back. Far from it!
Stealing the Gunderson account from you was merely a humble attempt on my part to simplify the
confusing array of life-choices which the Infinite Cosmos offers you every day!"

A MEANINGLESS COINCIDENCE.

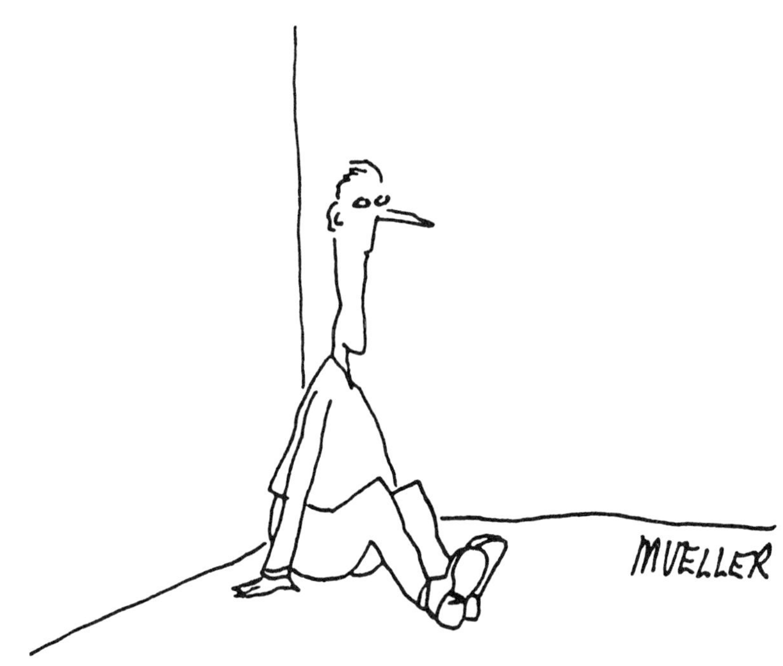

EXISTENTIAL FURNITURE.

THE TRUTH BROTHERS

UGLY.

AWFUL.

SIMPLE.

25 Years of Mr. Smiley Face: A Retrospective of His Life and Times...

I HEAR VOICES
IN MY HEAD
THAT TELL ME
TO DANCE.

EGO
SUPER-
EGO
VELEY
PREMIUM
SUPER-EGO
(HIGH PERFORMANCE)

BLESSING IN DISGUISE

"Me venomous? Heavens, no! Sarcastic, *maybe*, but that's only when I'm really ticked off!"

I'VE GOT TO GO NOW.
IT FEELS LIKE SOMEONE
IS MAKING A FIST
INSIDE MY SKULL.
MUELLER

Crafty Herb Cunningham gives Death the slip.

THE PEAS WHICH PASSETH ALL UNDERSTANDING.

You asked for them... Now here they are:
NEW AGE OFFICE SUPPLIES! ™
Our JUMBO PAPER CLIPS are lovingly hand-crafted, using metallic ores that were humanely removed from the earth only after we were absolutely sure it was what they really wanted. Box of 10: $29.95
Reduced to $225.00
COSMIC STAPLER. This addition to our catalogue joins paper together non-violently, by selecting only those sheets that have compatible auras. $325.00 includes shipping!
The MEDITATIVE PENCIL SHARPENER emits a slightly varying, gently repetitive background ambience perfect for any office environment.
A GUILT-FREE PAPER PUNCH? It's true!! Because it really doesn't "punch", per se... rather, it allows you to create exciting new space in each sheet. Call for latest price!
VELEY

THE BANALITY OF EVIL.

MUELLER

BOB FINDS HIMSELF

THE NEW WAVE.

Giving the devil his do.

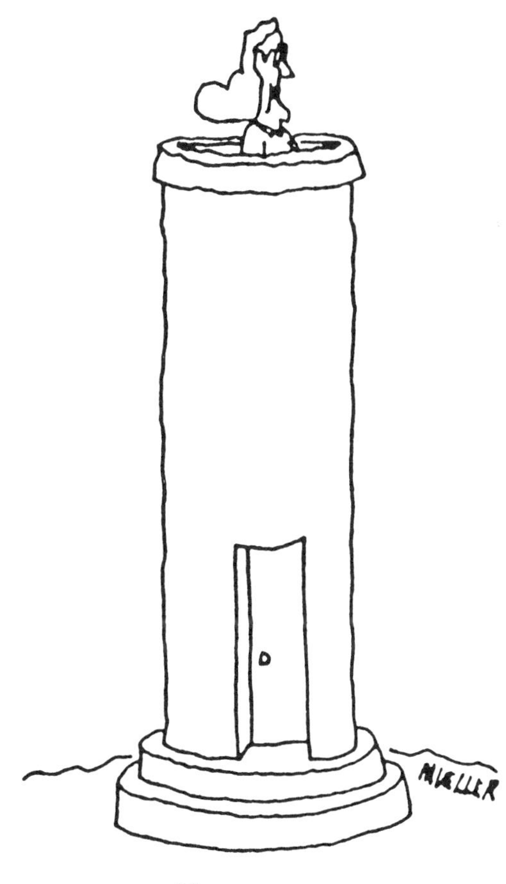

THE TOWER OF MABEL.

BEING AND
SOMETHINGNESS
MUELLER

Someday, Mister Nicky Copernicus, someday you'll learn that the world doesn't revolve around you!

BORN AGAIN

AND
AGAIN.
AND
AGAIN.
AND AGAIN.
AND
AGAIN
I HOPE
GOD CAN
HANDLE ALL
THOSE
STRETCH-
MARKS.

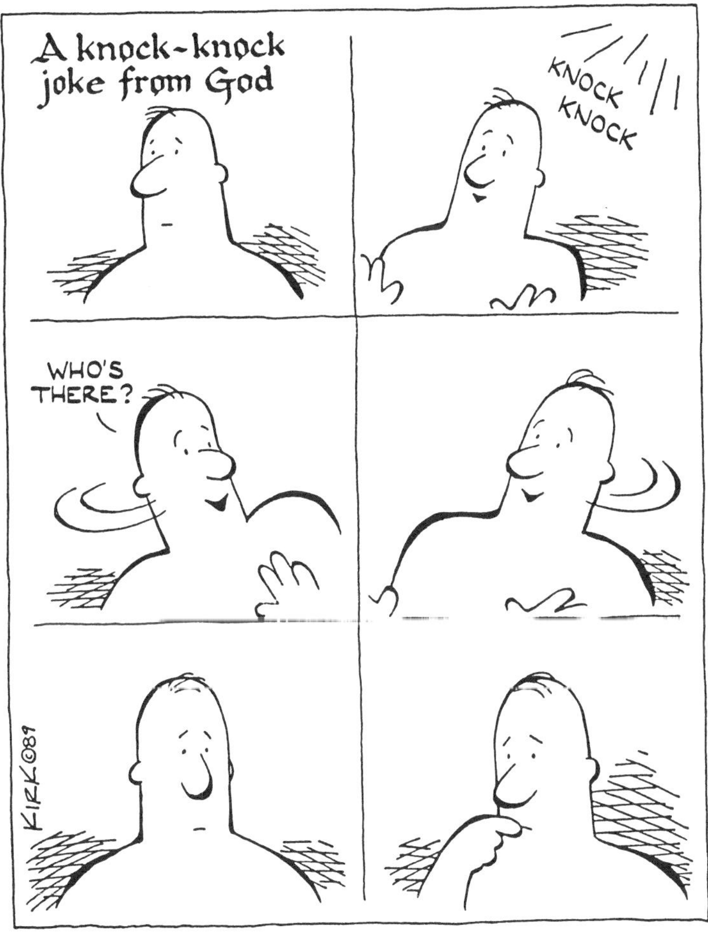
A knock-knock joke from God
KNOCK KNOCK
WHO'S THERE?
KIRK ©89

CREATIONIST RESEARCH.

Am I way off base, Phil, or am I hearing a little anger?

LITTLE KARMA SUNSHINE JOHNSON ON HER EIGHTEENTH BIRTHDAY.

NEW AGE FRAUDS. BY P.G. MUELLER

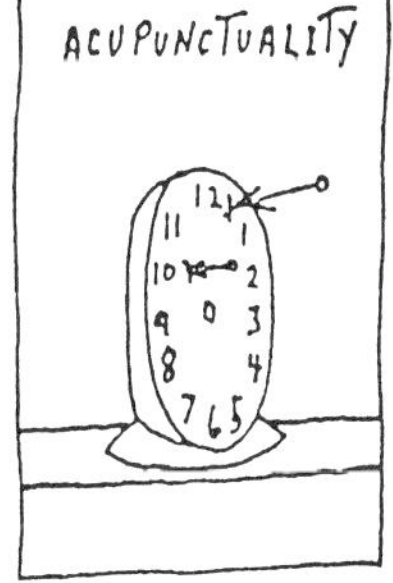

VELEY
Stein & Smith,
Psychiatrists
"Let us put wheels
on your
emotional baggage!"

UNCONVENTIONAL FORCES.
MUELLER

"Here, try these. They'll tastefully announce your return to the idealism of the '60s without any apologies for what you might've done in the '80s!"

SECULAR HOLY DAYS.
THE DAY OF THE IMMACULATE CONSUMPTION.
CRUNCH!
ZZZZZZZZZ...
THE DAY OF THE RIDICULOUS CONTRAPTION.
THE DAY OF THE PARTICULATE CONNIPTION.
THE DAY OF THE SPECTACULAR PRESCRIPTION.
P.S. MUELLER

PREACHING TO THE INVERTED
VELEY

THAT'LL BE ABOUT TWO WEEKS ON THE HUMANS, GOD. THEY'RE IN THE SHOP BEING PROGRAMMED FOR DOMINANCE AND WAR
okey doke...
BOB'S Planet Accessories
animals · forests · firmament and more
CREATIONISM WITH A DASH OF PLANNED OBSOLESCENCE
KIRK

STAIRWAY TO HEAVEN:
THE EXERCISE VIDEO.

"NEW AGE" MUSIC
CLAIMS ANOTHER VICTIM...

VELEY

THE EMPEROR HAS NO STYLE!
MUELLER

*Satan relaxing at home with the hounds of Hell
and his favorite media consultant.*

THE DAWN OF CIVILIZATION.

SOME MORE DEEP-SEATED AMERICAN VALUES
RELIGION
FAMILY
PATRIOTISM
VELEY

"Don't worry; it's only the fruit of conjecture."

Great.
No instructions.
That's just
great.
BUILD YOUR OWN
ANALYTICAL
MIND
KIRK

CHAOS
OUT OF ORDER.
MUELLER

Familiarity tries, unsuccessfully, to breed contempt in the lab.

NOT WITH A BANG BUT A HAMPER.

Support group for male Black Widow Spiders.

SURVIVAL OF THE FLATTEST.
MUELLER

When you're just Too Busy to consider the consequences of your actions, put your trust in:
ETHICS-GUARD SOFTWARE PRODUCTS TM
:Ahem: Excuse me! That stock transfer you're conducting sure isn't very nice, is it? After all, Ed is your best friend, right? But hey, I know you'll do what's right!
Thanks, Ethics-Guard!

EDNA FINDS THE HOLY GRAIL
WHILE CLEANING HER ATTIC

BORN UNDER A BAD SIGN

GREED
THE
CATALOG
MANY
NEW ITEMS!

A WISE MAN.

A JUST MAN.

A REGULAR GUY.

MUELLER

OPEN
THE POST-MODERN BAR & GRILL
SPECIALS:
EXISTENTIAL HOUR: 4-6
JADED PESSIMISM HOUR: 6-8
DECLINE OF WESTERN CIVILIZATION ASSUMED AS A GIVEN HOUR: 8-12
DELEY

CORPORATE - SPONSORED BAPTISM

CRITICAL MASS.
MUELLER

Bigfoot and the Loch Ness Monster have some fun with the tourists...

I WAS A SLUG
IN MY PREVIOUS LIFE, TOO!

SKIPPER FINDS HIMSELF AT A MORAL CROSSROADS...
VELEY

CONFESSIONAL MEGALOMANIA.
KNOW·IT·ALL!
MUELLER

AND NOW, FOR THE 12" PIZZA, WHAT IS THE TRUE NATURE OF REALITY? I'LL TAKE THE NINTH CORRECT CALLER...
RAMONES
KIRK
©90

"*I told you six months ago this might happen if you didn't get that disgusting little mole removed, but did you listen? Nooooo!*"

PLAY GOD! 50¢

I'M A PEOPLE-PERSON!
YOU'RE MY KIND OF PEOPLE!
WHAT A COMBINATION...
ME & YOU, US & US...
WE'RE PEOPLE-PERSONS!
AND SO ARE YOU!
A REAL CONFLAGRATION!
LET'S HAVE LUNCH!
VELEY
THE LEAST DANGEROUS CULT IN THE U.S.

In what year did Jesus Christ leave the carpentry trade?

What were the market principles underlying the Last Supper?

Compare the literary styles of the New Testament and Beowulf.

IF RELIGION WAS TAUGHT IN THE SCHOOLS

THE SEPARATION OF CHURCH AND STAN.
MUELLER

The Buck Stops Here:
I can only stay a few minutes today, Herb.
No prob, Phil. I know how busy you've been!

TRY TO THINK OF THIS
AS A SUPPORT GROUP
FOR THE ETERNALLY DAMNED.

MUELLER

Whoeeee!
7th Heaven
Ha Ha Ha Ha!!
What a riot!
Hey, turn the music up a bit!
3rd Heaven
VELEY

SEMI-ANNUAL LEAP OF FAITH.

Stan G.: A guy who learned everything he needed to know in Kindergarten.
If you whine enough, you'll eventually get what you want.
Sharing is for suckers.
Because I'm bigger than you, that's why.
Oh, yeah? You and what army?
If you tell on me, I'll tell on you.
VELEY

BAD
IDEAS
SELF DISCOVERY.
YOU ARE
HER. ↓
P.S. MUELLER

BEELZEBUBBLES.

KIRK ANDERSON

Kirk Anderson grew up in the dairy state, next to a cheese shop with a large statue of a talking cow, which he mistook for a religious shrine. He's been somewhat confused ever since. In adolescence he developed his first philosophy of life, "If you can't say something nice about someone, it's probably because they're a pathetic incompetent scum-sucking boob." During years of theological study he pruned his philosophy down to two words: "Be nice." He tried to parlay them into an inspirational self-help book, but felt that adding anything would simply water down his message. He reluctantly wrote Being and Niceness, as an attack on Sartre's famous work. It was a commercial flop.

This setback, however, did not prevent Kirk from acquiring experience and a college education. As the writer, illustrator, and salesperson for Super-Bee Comics, Kirk began to make his entrepreneurial mark way back in the fourth grade. Setting himself in the career track early on allowed Kirk to become the eventual owner and operator of Shameless Agitator T-Shirts (he always was the one to hop on the bandwagon of any cause that was worth making fun of). Soon there was no stopping the demand for his cartoons and illustrations. The Charles M. Schulz award was dropped at his feet. Others followed.

Kirk's current spiritual quest is to find a philosophy of life simple enough to fit on a bumper sticker and cute enough to mass market.

SELF-PORTRAIT OF KIRK ANDERSON'S GUARDIAN ANGEL, DOUG.

P.S. MUELLER

P.S. Mueller offers a timeline and explanation of his twisted path to fame.

1951: Born.

1952: Don't remember much.

1953: I was frightened by the leering television image of Pinky Lee, and to this day I am phobic in the presence of grown men wearing funny clothes.

1954: I began to realize, vaguely, that I was in Ohio.

1955: My first cartoon, captioned, "Poo poo on the Potomac."

1956: Dad started explaining *New Yorker* cartoons to me and Mom started explaining Dad.

1957: I got my first two-wheel bike and a bloody nose from Nancy Plunkett. Ever since, I have never denied a girl's request for the use of my bike.

1958: I listened to Stan Freberg records in the basement and read *Mad Magazine*.

1959: I plotted, drew, and lay in wait for the '60s.

1960: Thurber would be dead soon.

1961: I began to realize I had a lot of work to do and only fifth grade reading skills with which to do it. And on top of all that, we moved to a northern suburb of Chicago, where I met the Beaudry brothers, who introduced me to the heady pleasures of vandalism. Somewhat distracted by it all, I struggled vainly to draw.

1962: The Beaudry brothers told me about the human sex act and I laughed in their faces. The Kennedys were building Camelot and we were tearing down the neighborhood.

1963: I developed a crush on the White twins but couldn't tell them apart, and so repressed my feelings. My cartoon output dwindled.

1964: A good year for rock and roll but a strange year for Mueller. The White twins began their guest appearances in my Pinky Lee nightmares. I rocked and waited.

1965: I entered a Jesuit-run high school, a scary place, but the

Beaudry brothers had taught me stealth.

1966: I took a part time job in a tavern and my boss, Teddy Bear, introduced me to whisky and tobacco. A major leap forward in cartoon research.

1967: One day in study hall a scholastic confiscated some of my cartoons, and upon reading them, began to laugh uncontrollably. Things were looking up.

1968: First published cartoon, in the corporate newsletter for Ingersoll Steel.

1969: College and a regular cartoon spot on the editorial pages of the campus daily.

1970: I was elected to the student senate in the spring. Riots broke out. The Panthers went crazy. The S.D.S. went crazy. The state police went crazy. The school was closed early. I certainly hope it wasn't my fault.

1971: Dropped out and moved to California, possibly in search of the White twins. I starved and lived in a garret.

1972: I moved back to northern Illinois and took a job with a tropical plant rentals outfit. I'm the guy who put the marijuana seeds in the Chicago Crime Commissioner's desk planter.

1973: Worked at the greenhouse 10, 12 hours a day, six and seven days a week. They hated me and promoted me to operations manager. A German guy who worked for me was one of the people who bombed London during the war. I continued to draw in spite of everything, and began running editorial cartoons in the Libertyville *Independent Register*.

1974: Nixon and I resigned our respective offices. I don't know where he went, but I went back to college to major in English and starve elegantly.

1975: Starved elegantly.

1976: Graduated and starved inelegantly.

1977: My descent into radio. I was hired to write, produce, and voice commercials for WTAO-FM in Murphysboro, Illinois. It was an accident I tell you! I also contributed to the short-lived *non-Sequitur Magazine*.

1978: The radio station caught fire and I put it out. A mistake, but I needed the job at the time.

1979: A great year. I left the radio station and began drawing for the *Chicago Reader*.

1980: Moved to Madison, Wisconsin, and OOPS ... back to radio again, hosting an all night free-form music show.

1981: A fascist with a format reduced my job to less than factory work and I jumped ship to another station, where I wrote and produced commercials for WMAD-FM and WERU-AM.

1982. Commercials and cartoons. Hundreds of each.

1983: Promoted, if you can call it that, to the midday host on the AM station. But the whole place was a desperate nepotistic zoo. I plotted my departure from show business.

1984: I left radio and hibernated for a

year, drawing, building my cartoon empire.

1985: Suddenly I was discovered. Papers that wouldn't touch my work before were calling ME!

1986: Pee Wee Herman completely desensitized me out of the Pinky Lee Syndrome. Published first book of cartoons, *The Spread of Terror.*

1987: Bought a house on the east side of Madison. Turned into a cross between Dagwood and William Bendix. Most of the year was spent trying to fix a leak in my roof.

1988: Met a fascinating woman and was caught off guard by The Slap Of Love.

1989: Got married in late winter and awaited the release of my second book, *Playing Fast and Loose with Time and Space.*

1990: At this moment my wife is up on the roof with a bucket of tar and I'm working on a cartoon about the effects of laughter on the ozone layer. Don't know what I'll do if she fixes the leak.

BRADFORD VELEY

When the folks at *B&R* asked me to prepare this biographic sketch, my first reaction was "Great. My resume reads like I've got the attention span of an under-achieving cocker spaniel. What the hell am I going to say?" And then they told me not to be too obsessive about sticking to the facts. "Facts can obscure the truth," they said, and my heart leapt.

But where to begin? I suppose I could prattle on about all the transcendental experiences I've always wanted to have but probably never will. Or about my leeriness of organized religions (or disorganized ones, for that matter). But it'd just be the same boring laundry list of gripes, pseudo-epiphanies and metaphysical "to-dos" you've heard before, *ad nauseum.* And to be honest, it's hard for a guy who grew up in Iowa, the throbbing aorta of America's heartland, to talk so much about himself, even in the third person. Really, it's very painful.

That's when I decided to write about Martin Luther. You see, he and I go

123

way back. It all started when I found myself attending, of all places, Luther College, a lovely little school in Decorah (Iowa, of course). Now, I had been raised a teflon Presbyterian (they tried, but couldn't get it to stick), and I have to admit to mild surprise when I found myself enrolled at a church-affiliated school. But that was only the beginning.

As everybody knows, the number one problem with watershed events in your life, or even talking about them, is that if you're not properly dressed, you can get pretty darned wet. And who needs another lousy headcold, right? Which is exactly what I got that frozen homecoming night I spent protecting Martin Luther (well, his statue, anyway) from the slings, arrows, and outrageous spray paint of our slimy, dim-witted arch-rivals from St. Olaf College.

Statue patrol. It was such a dumb, thankless job that only freshmen were stupid enough to be talked into doing it. And so there I was, the quintessential freshman patsy, all alone and shivering in the stinging rain, grimly pondering my own short existence. "What's it all about?" I asked, to nobody in particular. "Is there any reason for all this suffering?" (I stole that one from an Ingmar Bergman movie). "Is God just basically an insensitive jerk?" (That was mine). And "Why am I here, and not taking extension courses at Tahiti Community College?"

And then the most miraculous thing happened. I looked up at the towering presence of our most famous constipated philosopher and I noticed he had flecks of paint on the insides of his bronze nostrils. Different colors, too. He had *already* been defiled, probably many times. My mission was beginning to assume a futile tinge. Crawling up and peering into those wise, baleful eyes, I looked for a sign. And suddenly it hit me how stupid this was. I'm what?—expecting a statue, at four in the morning, *a statue with spray-paint up his nose*, to tell me what life is all about? This was Iowa, remember, *before* "Field of Dreams." That's when I decided to go home to bed.

So I did. And that night I decided two things. I decided that, given a choice, I'd take warm and dry over wet, miserable and waiting to be enlightened. *Any* day.

OK, so it hasn't always worked out that way—sometimes enlightenment just knocks down your door and elbows its way inside, no matter how hard you fight it—but all in all, things have been just fine. Oh, I almost forgot: I also decided to become a cartoonist that night, but that's a different story altogether. At present, I live in Michigan with my wife, Faith Ann, and our two children, but I still dream about Iowa.